D0629185

**ALSO BY ELLIS WEINER AND BARBARA DAVILMAN**

*How to Profit from the Coming Rapture*

*How to Raise a Jewish Dog*

*Yiddish with George and Laura*

*Yiddish with Dick and Jane*

**ALSO BY ELLIS WEINER**

*The Joy of Worry*

*Drop Dead, My Lovely*

*The Big Boat to Bye-Bye*

*Santa Lives! Five Conclusive Arguments for the
Existence of Santa Claus*

**ALSO BY BARBARA DAVILMAN (WITH LIZ DUBELMAN)**

*What Was I Thinking: 58 Bad Boyfriend Stories*

# ARFFIRMATIONS

## MEDITATIONS

## FOR

## YOUR DOG

ELLIS WEINER AND BARBARA DAVILMAN

Photographs by Susan Burnstine

ST. MARTIN'S PRESS

NEW YORK

TO ALL ANIMAL RESCUE GROUPS AROUND THE COUNTRY,
WHOSE TIRELESS WORK SAVES LIVES EVERY DAY.

AND TO THE MEMORY OF COPPER, WHO IN OUR
HEARTS WILL ALWAYS BE BAYING AT POSSUMS
AND GOBBLING UP ALL THE LOX.

ARFFIRMATIONS. Copyright © 2008 by Ellis Weiner and Barbara
Davilman. All rights reserved. Printed in the United States of
America. For information, address St. Martin's Press, 175 Fifth
Avenue, New York, N.Y. 10010.

All photos by Susan Burnstine

www.stmartins.com

Library of Congress Cataloging-in-Publication Data

Weiner, Ellis.
   Arffirmations : meditations for your dog / Ellis Weiner and Barbara
Davilman.—1st ed.
      p. cm.
   ISBN-13: 978-0-312-38704-4
   ISBN-10: 0-312-38704-0
   1. Dogs—Humor. 2. Meditations—Humor. I. Davilman, Barbara.
II. Title.
PN6231.D68W438  2009
818'.5402—dc22

                                                    2008029875

First Edition: January 2009

10   9   8   7   6   5   4   3   2   1

# CONTENTS

Arffirmations are positive statements of confidence, empowerment, and purpose. When properly used, they can be effective in neutralizing or even preventing those feelings of guilt, shame, or embarrassment you get when you do something your owner doesn't want you to do.

Arffirmations provide inspiration and spiritual uplift, regardless of your age, gender, or breed. If you prefer, you may read them silently to yourself. However, Arffirmations are much more effective if barked out loud.

Simply browse through these pages until you come upon a topic that has meaning to you and to your own personal life. Read the Arffirmation and concentrate on the meaning of the ideas being expressed.

Repeat this process for several days, and you will discover a remarkable thing: You will be able to indulge in behavior your owner doesn't like, without experiencing any of the old negative feelings that may previously have accompanied or followed it.

It seems like magic, but it's actually based on established, proven, psychological and spiritual principles. By reading Arffirmations, we consciously tell our unconscious mind that everything we do is spiritually enlightened and cosmically benign and okay. In this way we reprogram our minds to stop making us feel guilty, inadequate, or wrong. By telling ourselves how good we are, we can learn to ignore it when our owner tells us how bad we are.

Commit to reading (and really *pondering* and *understanding*) these Arffirmations, and they will change the way you think, not only about tail-chasing, poop-eating, and endless, "unnecessary" barking, but—more importantly—about yourself.

I

# ARFFIRMATIONS

# FOR

# SPIRITUAL

# INSIGHT

ARFFIRMATIONS FOR SPIRITUAL INSIGHT

## I AM PERFECT
## AND AM TREATED ACCORDINGLY

I am one with the Wisdom that emanates in Love from the Power at the heart of Life. This knowledge makes me quietly secure in the awareness that I can accomplish anything I choose to concentrate on. Therefore I concentrate on being perfect. I do this, not only for my own sake but for the sake of others. When others see my perfection, they are inspired. They are uplifted. They give me a cookie.

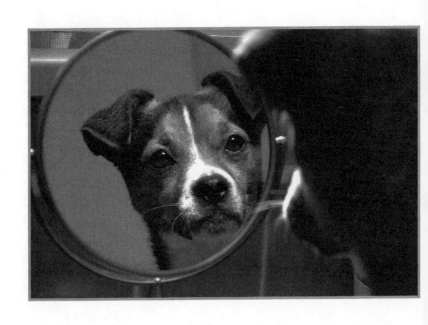

ARFFIRMATIONS FOR SPIRITUAL INSIGHT

## WHEN I GAZE INTO THE MIRROR,
## I REJOICE IN THE ME-NESS OF ME

Purebreds resemble only one another. I, on the other hand, resemble millions. I look into the mirror to remind myself of this. I look to confirm that I am all dogs, and all dogs are me. I also look to see if I am getting any gray hairs. And each time I look, I am reminded that I am fascinating.

ARFFIRMATIONS FOR SPIRITUAL INSIGHT

## SIZE IS A STATE OF MIND

It is not that I am "small on the outside but big on the inside." I am small on the inside, too—but only physically. My heart is gigantic, my mind is immense, and my soul is huge. On occasion my enormous spirit feels cramped in this miniature body, and my expression at times reflects this discomfort. Still, I bear it with dignity. No single body, of any kind, can hope to contain a personality as vast as mine. When I give voice to this truth, some call it "attitude." I call it "living from the inside out."

ARFFIRMATIONS FOR SPIRITUAL INSIGHT

## I DEVOTEDLY PERFORM SPIRITUAL EXERCISES
## FOR THE BENEFIT OF MYSELF AND OTHERS

To the unenlightened, it may appear that I am begging. In reality I am practicing my practice. This posture is part of the sequence called "Salutation to the Sun." I assume these poses daily, usually in the presence of humans eating at the kitchen table. In this way I clear my *doggie chi.* I inspire those eating nearby to clear *their* chi by giving me leftovers. In this way we join together as One: pure, whole, centered, aware, and fed.

ARFFIRMATIONS FOR SPIRITUAL INSIGHT

## I AM PRESENT IN MY MIND WITH MY BODY, AND VICE VERSA

In the maintenance of my physical body, I have learned to adopt various positions to help my inner energy flow in the most life-enhancing ways. By crossing my paws, I balance the polarities of left and right. By thinking about my crossed paws, I encourage the rest of me to align along an axis of body consciousness. The same idea is behind other positions I assume, including lying on the bed with my head hanging off the edge, and sticking my rear foot into one of my ears.

ARFFIRMATIONS FOR SPIRITUAL INSIGHT

## I AM A PURE SPIRIT SO IT DOESN'T MATTER
## WHAT THEY MAKE ME WEAR

Looking within, I see the profound truth of the infinite soul that lies at the heart of my being. My essence is eternal and my wholeness is unique. Compared to this unquestionable reality, what do I care if they make me wear a silly pink outfit with a hood? Or that red sweater that what's-her-name crocheted, or even those reindeer antlers every Christmas? I am secure in my inner perfection.

2

# ARFFIRMATIONS

# FOR

# INTROSPECTION

ARFFIRMATIONS FOR INTROSPECTION

## I TAKE THE TIME TO REJOICE
## IN MY WONDERFUL WORLD

No matter how hectic my daily routine—from barking at the mailman to announcing visitors to licking myself for half an hour straight—I am never too busy to pause to appreciate my life. I lie back, take stock, and count my blessings. I reflect with satisfaction on how much I've grown spiritually and emotionally. I direct my awareness to the softness of the grass. I focus my attention on the beauty of the sky and of the foliage around me. And I consciously keep an eye on the squirrels. When the time comes for me to tell them where to go, I am always ready.

ARFFIRMATIONS FOR INTROSPECTION

## MY HAIR IS A GIFT
## I SHARE WITH THE WORLD

The wisdom of the ages is to be found in my coat's distinctive, tight coils. From this I derive my great intelligence. It is my obligation to go out in the world and share this gift with others. This is how I fulfill my Destiny. This is also how I "give back"—by allowing others to admire me.

ARFFIRMATIONS FOR INTROSPECTION

## I BURY THINGS SO THAT THE UNIVERSE
## CANNOT FIND THEM

Peace. Protection. Security. I obtain all these and more when I bury objects that are precious to me. In concealing their whereabouts from other dogs, humans, and, of course, cats, I affirm my authority over what is mine. Only I know their locations. These are my secrets. Secrets imbue me with mystery and importance. Secrets make me sexy.

ARFFIRMATIONS FOR INTROSPECTION

## MY WHEEZY SNORING IS THE MUSIC
## OF REPLENISHMENT AND RENEWAL

*M*other Nature in her infinite wisdom has endowed me with a very big head, because I carry around very big thoughts. When my load of thoughts gets overwhelmingly heavy, I must sleep. It is then that I connect with the One Infinite Mind. It is all-knowing. It is all-seeing. It is all-hearing. It is all-smelling. When I surrender to slumber, I connect to that original source of energy and love, which restores my body and rejuvenates my soul. The noises I make while sleeping are the sound track to the movie that is my inner life.

ARFFIRMATIONS FOR INTROSPECTION

## I GRACEFULLY ACCEPT THE FACT THAT
## MY CUTENESS IS A METAPHYSICAL REALITY

I am fully aware that the world thinks I'm unbelievably cute. The human response to my adorableness (the cooing, the squealing, the gasps of awe) are the normal sounds of my environment. It is a condition I accept with grace and ease—just as those around me accept, with similar grace and ease, the sound of me incessantly yapping my head off for absolutely no reason whatsoever.

# 3

# ARFFIRMATIONS FOR ATTRACTING AND ACCEPTING FOOD

ARFFIRMATIONS FOR ATTRACTING AND ACCEPTING FOOD

## I WANT TO EAT EVERYTHING,
## AND EVERYTHING WANTS ME TO EAT IT

In the cycle of Life, everything has a purpose. Food exists to be eaten. I exist for a purpose, too: I exist to eat. Humans exist in order to give me food, so that I can eat. Therefore, by expressing my interest in your food, I affirm my, your, and its (the food's) purpose, and our place in this World. You eat; I beg; you feed me; I eat. This is the cycle in which each of us (plus the food) has a place. We are blessed to be enveloped in this miraculous and splendid reality. So just give me the food.

ARFFIRMATIONS FOR ATTRACTING AND ACCEPTING FOOD

## I AM PERFECT EVEN IF I DID
## EAT THAT MUFFIN SOMEBODY DROPPED
## NEAR THE DUMPSTER

I am an omnivore. Nothing edible is alien to me, although I do not care for raw garlic, green peppers, or, of course, lemons. But the ice cream that has fallen onto the sidewalk, the Cheerios some toddler has spilled along the way, the French fries cast upon a parking lot—most of which maybe a car has run over—all are fit sustenance for me. I desire to consume everything not nailed down because I am free and my appetite is as large as the universe.

ARFFIRMATIONS FOR ATTRACTING AND ACCEPTING FOOD

## I SALUTE MY WONDERFUL, MULTIFACETED
## NATURE WITH WHATEVER I EAT

*M*y diet expresses both my complex personality and what my soul hungers for. When I eat dog food, I demonstrate my need to connect with my ancestors. When I eat human food, I pay tribute to how much I love my humans, particularly their food. When I eat dead animals, grass, and dog poop, I glory in my desire to just gross everyone out.

ARFFIRMATIONS FOR ATTRACTING AND ACCEPTING FOOD

## AS A PREDATOR I MOVE CONFIDENTLY
## ACROSS THE FIELDS OF THE KITCHEN

I am a domesticated animal—but I am still an animal. My need for the hunt never goes away, and my methods remain unchanged over aeons. Only my quarry reflects my civilization-based lifestyle. Where I once, with my pack, pursued the deer of the forest or the bison of the plain, now all by myself I capture the hamburgers unguarded on the picnic table, the bagels displayed on a platter in the dining room, and the entire roast pork loin "resting" on the cutting board. Even when I spontaneously swipe the spaghetti and clam sauce when you go to answer the phone, I am engaged in, and one with, the hunt.

ARFFIRMATIONS FOR ATTRACTING AND ACCEPTING FOOD

## THE BREADTH OF MY TASTE IN FOOD
## REVEALS THE VASTNESS OF MY SPIRIT

Just as my soul is infinite in its scope, the range of my taste in food is without boundaries or limitations. It is for this reason that I pity humans, who will never know the delights and satisfactions of sampling used Kleenex or tampons. The universe of what I find edible is immense— and, like the physical universe, is expanding daily.

ARFFIRMATIONS FOR ATTRACTING AND ACCEPTING FOOD

## I DO NOT FEAR THE EMPTY FOOD BOWL
## BECAUSE I ENVISION AN ABUNDANCE OF
## TREATS IN MY LIFE

**M**y empty bowl does not cause me panic. I am surrounded by a remarkable variety of resources from which I may obtain delicious treats. From the carrot shreds that fly to the floor during the making of slaw, to the stale baguette sticking up from the kitchen garbage can; from the pretzels left unguarded in the den, to the crusts of the peanut butter and jelly sandwich abandoned on the patio; from the single-serving little bags of Doritos I secure from the kids even while they are actually eating from them while playing a video game, to the broccoli they smuggle to me under the table during dinner: I live in and with abundance. My bowl may be empty, but my world is full.

# 4

# ARFFIRMATIONS
# FOR REPLACING
# FEAR WITH FAITH

ARFFIRMATIONS FOR REPLACING FEAR WITH FAITH

## BEFORE THE BATH:

## I COURAGEOUSLY FACE LIFE'S MOST DIFFICULT

## CHALLENGES WITHOUT FEAR OR ANXIETY

Within the self of my being, I am whole and complete. No one and nothing can affect that. Therefore I am not bothered by petty annoyances, such as having to take a bath. The disturbing noise of the water, the slippery bottom of the tub that my paws cannot get traction on, the horrible splashing of the unnaturally warm wetness all over my body—I experience these things and say to myself, *Thank you, but I choose not to be petrified and nauseated.* Instead, I concentrate on future opportunities to get smelly and dirty all over again. Thus I am at ease and unperturbed no matter where I am in the cycle of hygiene.

ARFFIRMATIONS FOR REPLACING FEAR WITH FAITH

## AFTER THE BATH:

## MY DIGNITY IS UNAFFECTED

This is not at all humiliating. On the contrary, my inner uniqueness shines all the more brightly when my outer coat is wet. That is why I stand very still when being bathed: I am deep in thought, focusing on how, when it is over, I will spread my distinctive "wet dog" smell to every room in the house. Thus, those who bathe me are themselves bathed in my very Essence and smell.

ARFFIRMATIONS FOR REPLACING FEAR WITH FAITH

## I AM UNTHREATENED BY
## LOUD HOUSEHOLD APPLIANCES

This object does not frighten me—a fact I prove by turning my back on the device and venturing into the kitchen, where I help myself to whatever is within reach upon the counter. In this way I easily demonstrate that I am self-sufficient and able to cope with unpleasant cleaning apparatus. I am superb.

ARFFIRMATIONS FOR REPLACING FEAR WITH FAITH

## I RUN INSIDE AT THE SOUND OF THUNDER
## TO CELEBRATE SUDDEN EXPLOSIVE NOISES
## WITH INSPIRED WORKS OF ART

Why do I immediately run inside when I hear these unexpected noises? It is not to hide under the desk and tremble. On the contrary, I celebrate the sounds by dashing into the living room and banging into the coffee table. This, in turn, knocks all the candy out of the candy dish. The sweets make a beautiful pattern on the floor. With this arrangement of colors and shapes I express my inner feelings in an artistically gratifying creation that endures until, in a moment of reflection, I eat it. Then I spit out the wrappers into another artistically gratifying creation. In this way I am inspired by the thunder. I am one with the boom. I am at peace with Life, and with Life's booms, and with Life's candies.

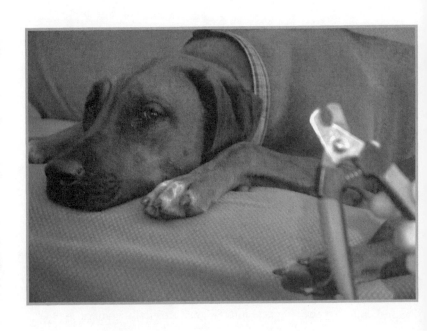

ARFFIRMATIONS FOR REPLACING FEAR WITH FAITH

## I TAKE RESPONSIBILITY FOR
## MY OWN FEELINGS WHEN
## THEY CLIP MY NAILS

I love my nails for the same reason as I love my tail: they extend my being out into the world. When, as sometimes happens, my nails are cut, I am diminished. My being is trimmed and my world is made smaller. But I take responsibility for reacting to this diminishment by eating certain select pieces of trash from the bathroom wastebasket and, often, leaving used dental floss all over the floor. This makes me feel whole and complete again.

ARFFIRMATIONS FOR REPLACING FEAR WITH FAITH

## I COPE SKILLFULLY WITH THE
## SOUNDS OF POPCORN BEING MICROWAVED

My ears are enormous and open to the universe. They hear everything, from the back of your earring falling onto the floor, to a petal dropping gently off a flower. But my great sensitivity can be a mixed blessing. When you microwave popcorn, it sounds to me like an automatic weapon being fired outside into a mattress. I respond by running back and forth in the den until the hideous din ceases. It is my way of reminding you that you'll need to stay on the treadmill an extra fifteen minutes if you want to burn off the result of that disturbingly noisy snack. I then regain my unshakeable poise.

# 5

# ARFFIRMATIONS
# FOR SELF-KNOWLEDGE

ARFFIRMATIONS FOR SELF-KNOWLEDGE

## WHEN I DRINK FROM THE TOILET
## I CELEBRATE MY UNIQUENESS

Water is the very source of Life. I desire and require the freshest source of water available. Why should I confine myself to the stagnant pool of tepid liquid that sits, accumulating crud, in my water dish, when the toilet refreshes and replenishes itself many times a day? The toilet is my personal fountain, fed by the mysterious sources of water beneath the home and rising up from below the surface of the earth. I deserve nothing less.

ARFFIRMATIONS FOR SELF-KNOWLEDGE

## MY SHEDDING IS AN ACT OF LOVE

**R**adiance. Spirit. Joy. These reside at the center of my Being, just as my Being is housed in my body. I inhabit my body fully, and my body inhabits my home fully. That is why I leave samples of my physical self for others to encounter. By shedding I announce to the world not only that "I was here, and fully present with love," but that "Even after I leave, part of me—equally present, equally loving—is *still* here."

ARFFIRMATIONS FOR SELF-KNOWLEDGE

## I FREELY EXPRESS THE JOY OF MY DESIRES
## BY DROOLING

I am light, energy, emotion, physical spirit, essence, and, yes—drool. Drool is the manifestation of desire when in the presence of nourishing foodstuffs. When it dribbles onto the kitchen table until you cry, "Oh, gross!" or when it leaves a wet stain on your lap, or when you slip and nearly break your neck sliding on a slick spot on the floor, I know that I am doing naturally what nature intended.

ARFFIRMATIONS FOR SELF-KNOWLEDGE

## MY INSIDE-OUT EARS SIGNAL THAT I HAVE BEEN CHASING MY TAIL IN AN ENDLESS QUEST THAT IS ONE WITH THE ETERNAL CYCLES OF ETERNITY

I do not chase my tail in order to catch it. The meaning of the journey is to be found not in the destination but in the journey itself. Therefore I chase my tail in order to chase it. When I am finished, my ears are inside out—a clear signal to those around me that I have undertaken my spiritual quest for the day. At those times everyone knows to allow me my "space" until I have recovered from the rigors of my inner discipline. When my ears fall back into their normal position, I may be approached and offered treats.

ARFFIRMATIONS FOR SELF-KNOWLEDGE

## I RUN BACK AND FORTH THROUGH THE LIVING ROOM LIKE A MANIAC BECAUSE I GLORY IN THE LOVE I HAVE FOR MYSELF

I am a creature of Divine Love and eternal spirit. Sometimes I forget that. But when I remember, the thought ignites my soul with energy, and I dash like a maniac all over my home. The result? A throw-rug is doubled-up, a brimming wastebasket is overturned, and a beautiful, precious vase is toppled and shattered—all in honor of my joyous celebration.

ARFFIRMATIONS FOR SELF-KNOWLEDGE

## I BARK OVER AND OVER FOR NO APPARENT REASON AND NEVER SHUT UP BECAUSE IT IS WHO I AM

I am at the center of the world, and I announce my presence to everyone and everything. Over and over. Without cease. Continually. Unbidden, unchecked, and unstopping. Who will proclaim my vital importance to all of existence if I do not? In this way I proclaim my love of myself and of my life to everyone in my environment.

# 6

# ARFFIRMATIONS FOR SELF-LOVE AND SELF-ACCEPTANCE

ARFFIRMATIONS FOR SELF-LOVE AND SELF-ACCEPTANCE

# I AM A SPLENDID AND SUPERB ALPHA AND IT IS OKAY IF I DESTROY CERTAIN PARTS OF YOUR LAWN

As an alpha dog, I am fully committed to my responsibility to pee on certain areas of grass or bushes in reply to the pees of previous dogs. When I do so, I ask myself, *Is this justified? Is it really okay, this peeing on a patch of grass that has already been extensively peed on and is now a burnt brown color instead of a lush, beautiful green?* But all I need to do is look within. There I discover the Inner Intelligence whose wisdom I always trust. It tells me, *Yes. It is your task. Pee where you will.* And I know that all is right in my world.

ARFFIRMATIONS FOR SELF-LOVE AND SELF-ACCEPTANCE

## I DISOBEY YOU BECAUSE I FULLY LOVE
## AND RESPECT MYSELF

*C*ome. Sit. Stay. Shut up. I openly do none of these things when told to. Granted, it is your path to command me to do them. But my path is different, and need not require obedience to being bossed around by you on your path. I am on an endless journey of self-discovery through Time and Space, and I easily release myself from the obligation to validate the limitations that others would place upon me. I need not come, nor sit, nor stay, nor shut up, because I am magnificent. And it is because I am magnificent that you can deny me nothing.

ARFFIRMATIONS FOR SELF-LOVE AND SELF-ACCEPTANCE

## I AFFIRM MY MAGNIFICENCE WHEN I
## PICK A FIGHT WITH EVERY BIG DOG I SEE

*M*y life is defined by abundance: almost all the dogs on earth are bigger than I am, and I yap and snarl at every one. If a dog barks back at me, I bark back even louder. If a dog does not bark back at me, I keep barking nonetheless. I do this willingly, relentlessly, and without provocation. I do it because my mind is connected to the One Divine Intelligence. Plus, I know they are jealous of my pearls. I could take my pearls off, but I will not do this. They define and complete me. Without them, I would lose the reason to bark, depriving me of both my purpose in life and my ability to enjoy the sound of my own voice.

ARFFIRMATIONS FOR SELF-LOVE AND SELF-ACCEPTANCE

## I DESERVE TO SIT ON THE SOFA

I am fully conscious of the rule forbidding me to be on this sofa. Nonetheless, I embrace my birthright to recline at ease on any piece of furniture in my home. I am free, calm, safe, and at peace. If, upon returning, you rebuke me for disobeying this stricture, I pretend to feel guilt and shame and embarrassment to please you. Then, once you leave, I proceed to get on the sofa again, to please me.

ARFFIRMATIONS FOR SELF-LOVE AND SELF-ACCEPTANCE

## MY REFUSAL TO GO OUT INTO THE RAIN
## DEMONSTRATES MY SELF-RESPECT

Sometimes, when it is raining, you call me to go for a walk, or even merely to step outside to pee. At those times, I respond as I must: with expression, body language, and mental visualization, I convey the only possible and correct reply, which is: *Forget it.* It is not simply that "I don't do rain." Rather, rain is anathema to me. Were I willingly to expose myself to falling water for the smallest moment of Time, even under the supposed shelter of your laughably inadequate umbrella, I would not be myself. Small wonder that, when you drag me outside, I return sulking. My self-esteem has gotten all wet, and I must wait until it dries out and returns to its normal radiance.

ARFFIRMATIONS FOR SELF-LOVE AND SELF-ACCEPTANCE

## BY CHEWING ON THE SEAT BELTS WHEN I RIDE IN THE CAR I AM ATTENTIVE TO THE MESSAGES OF MY BODY

I know that my body loves me, and I love it. As I look within, I am aware that my body sends me messages. I am receptive to them and strive to accommodate my body's needs. When riding in the backseat of your car, for example, I receive a message from my mouth. It says, *I need you to chew on the seat belt.* I do not hesitate to comply. By granting my body's requests, I am Whole.

# 7

# ARFFIRMATIONS FOR ATTAINING ENLIGHTENMENT

ARFFIRMATIONS FOR ATTAINING ENLIGHTENMENT

## I KNOW, AND I HAVE ALWAYS KNOWN, WHAT IS TRULY IMPORTANT

I cannot believe they paid $1.2 million for that house, and then tore it down to build something bigger. They believe such an extravagant act will make them happy, but I was born knowing that happiness is possible only where the spirit is free to expand. That can happen only in a dwelling devoid of the unnecessary. Four walls, a roof, and simple but fragrant wall-to-wall carpeting are all anyone—dog or human—needs. My own home gives testament to this truth.

ARFFIRMATIONS FOR ATTAINING ENLIGHTENMENT

## I EXPLORE MY WONDERFUL WORLD IN
## NEW AND ENLIGHTENING PLACES WHEN
## I REPEATEDLY RUN AWAY

Whether dashing through an open front door, tunneling under the fence on the side, or simply jumping over a short wall in the backyard, I go forth to expand my world every day. Be it next door, down the block, or in some godforsaken neighborhood across town, I know someone will find me. They will call my owner, who will come to retrieve me. And then the cycle will begin anew, in an endless round of escape, exploration, and retrieval. As I ride back to my owner's home I can tell she is excited to hear about my adventures. I can tell she is envious of my wanderlust and curiosity. I can tell she is just pretending to be pissed off at me.

ARFFIRMATIONS FOR ATTAINING ENLIGHTENMENT

## I FREELY SHARE MY ENLIGHTENMENT
## WITH OTHERS, EVEN THOSE SQUIRRELS

I make no judgment regarding those stupid squirrels as they gnaw on their silly nuts on that tree. Rather, I am centered, calm, and at peace even in their presence. In fact, I willingly share with them the valuable Wisdom I have gained from Life. I do this in my characteristic bay, to be sure that they (and other animals, and humans, and cats in the vicinity) can hear me. And I thoughtfully repeat myself over and over, to make sure they get the message. It is a message of joy. It is a message of love. It is my greeting and benediction to all squirrels, everywhere. I know they hear me.

ARFFIRMATIONS FOR ATTAINING ENLIGHTENMENT

## I AM ALWAYS IN THE RIGHT PLACE,
## EVEN IN THE CAR

No one knows better than I that objects in the mirror may appear smaller than their actual size, because I always ride shotgun. I don't even have to "call it," because all know it is my right, my duty, and my Destiny. From that vantage point I am easily able to crawl into the driver's lap and create provocative hieroglyphs on the window with my nose. And if the window happens to be open, I am able to poke my head outside and greet other drivers. They happily acknowledge that I am where I should be.

ARFFIRMATIONS FOR ATTAINING ENLIGHTENMENT

## I UNITE TWO WORLDS WHEN I BURY BONES OR COOKIES AND THEN DIG THEM UP AND THEN REBURY THEM IN THE SOFA

I live inside, yes, but I also go outside because I am an animal. I am a part of Nature—and Nature is outside. Thus, inside and outside come together in me. When I take something from inside outside and then bring it inside with little pieces of outside on it, I am expressing fully the totality of my being. I am wondrous. I am Yin and Yang. Sitting on the sofa, eating a dirt-encrusted cookie, I am Whole.

# 8

# ARFFIRMATIONS FOR PROTECTION AND SAFETY

ARFFIRMATIONS FOR PROTECTION AND SAFETY

## I BARK AT PEOPLE WALKING PAST MY HOUSE
## IN CELEBRATION AND WARNING

I occupy this home with love and commitment. These feelings extend out from me in all directions, including into the front yard and into the street and halfway down the block. When people walk past, I celebrate their entering into my Field of Concern with barking and whining and jumping around. In this way, the whole world knows that I know that they are there. No one who moves past the home can fail to understand that I am vigilant—and wonderful.

ARFFIRMATIONS FOR PROTECTION AND SAFETY

## I DILIGENTLY ASSESS YOU WHEN YOU
## TRY TO COME INSIDE

Friend or foe? I will be the judge of that. True, my expression does not change. To the unenlightened it appears that I am full of bitterness and resentment. But in reality I am motivated by Love—for my humans, for myself, and for Life. Do I sense that you bring peace, harmony, and radiant joy? Then you are welcome. Do you live in fear and wallow in chaos, and engender strife and discord? Then to you I say, *Back off*.

ARFFIRMATIONS FOR PROTECTION AND SAFETY

## I UNLEASH COSMIC POWER WHEN
## I BARK AT THE UPS TRUCK

Each time I bark, I change the universe. And there is ample evidence of my power. The drivers of delivery trucks need not even stop or approach my home in order to hear—and heed—my warning. The cosmos itself conveys my message, and they (usually) just keep driving. I am invincible.

ARFFIRMATIONS FOR PROTECTION AND SAFETY

## WE PRAISE OURSELVES WHEN
## WE REPEL THE MAILMAN

We applaud our ability to protect the home and the family by warding off this invader. We are too clever to be distracted by the printed objects he leaves. We glory in these triumphs and we are fully aware of how wonderful we are—just as we once did with the bottled water delivery guy, whom we chased away after a single visit. He now dares to come only once a month. We are alert, fearless, and always on duty (except for Sundays).

# 9

# ARFFIRMATIONS FOR
# DOG—HUMAN HARMONY

ARFFIRMATIONS FOR DOG-HUMAN HARMONY

## BY FETCHING EVERY TENNIS BALL I SEE, INCLUDING THOSE WITH WHICH PEOPLE ARE ACTUALLY PLAYING TENNIS, I REALIZE MY UNLIMITED POTENTIAL

This—the fetching of tennis balls—is my job, and I apply myself to it with loving commitment. I know that the more I pursue my responsibilities with energy and creativity, the more the universe itself will reward me with bounty. When humans respond to my efforts with cries of "Hey! Bring that back!" and "Put that down!" I know that everything in my world is as it should be.

ARFFIRMATIONS FOR DOG-HUMAN HARMONY

## I SHOW SAINTLY PATIENCE WAITING
## FOR THE POOL MAN TO FINISH

As a Lab, I know, and the world knows, that I was born to swim. It is what the Universe wants me to do. For me not to swim is to go against Nature. But even I cannot swim when the pool man performs his necessary activities every week. At those times I demonstrate my capacity for deep calm and spiritual poise. I am centered, perfect, and at peace in the Now, and almost completely unperturbed by his foul-smelling chemicals and the net with the menacing long handle. Then, when he finally leaves, I imbue the sacred waters with my Essence once again.

ARFFIRMATIONS FOR DOG-HUMAN HARMONY

## I SNARL AT YOUR JERKY BOYFRIEND
## OUT OF LOVE

When I see he is here again I empower myself to express my innermost thoughts and feelings. I know, with a deep understanding, that he cannot be better to sleep with than I am. Yet, I do not judge, for I choose to live without negativity. Rather, I am content to love and embrace you until you are able to love and embrace yourself, and no longer allow that schmuck to treat you like a doormat.

ARFFIRMATIONS FOR DOG-HUMAN HARMONY

## I GLORY IN MY WONDERFUL WORLD WHEN
## I BURY MY NOSE IN THE CROTCHES OF VISITORS

*M*y nose is my most sensitive organ. I sense that the same is true of the human crotch. That is why I introduce my snout into a visitor's most treasured area of privacy: as a greeting, as a gesture of welcome, and as an act of communion between fellow animals. My world is lovingly populated by those who smell and those who are smelled.

ARFFIRMATIONS FOR DOG-HUMAN HARMONY

## I GIFT YOU YOUR OWN SOCK
### *BECAUSE* IT IS YOURS

How wonderful it is that I give myself permission to present you with your own sock when you return from work. It is with joy that I deposit your own slipper on the bed when you are out shopping, to await you when you get back. I embody Love when I run about with your shoe in my mouth when you come home from shopping. I do these things because I am confident that such items have value to you. I applaud my ability not to give you someone *else's* footwear.

ARFFIRMATIONS FOR DOG-HUMAN HARMONY

## I WHINE WHEN YOU LEAVE THE HOME
## BECAUSE I KNOW HOW MUCH YOU WILL MISS ME

Why do I whimper every single time you walk out the door, even just to get the paper? It is because I am blessed with empathic sensitivity. I know, even before you leave, how much you will wish you were back home, glorying in the magnificence that is I. It is only natural and fitting that you feel this way. I know, as you know, that I am the cutest thing in the universe. I combine adorableness and genius. If I were not myself, I would miss me, too.

Ellis Weiner and Barbara Davilman are authors of *Yiddish with Dick and Jane, Yiddish with George and Laura, How to Raise a Jewish Dog,* and *How to Profit from the Coming Rapture.*

Ellis is the author of *The Joy of Worry, Drop Dead, My Lovely, The Big Boat to Bye-Bye,* and *Santa Lives!: Five Conclusive Arguments for the Existence of Santa Claus.*

Barbara is editor, along with Liz Dubelman, of *What Was I Thinking?*